12/03

U.S. ★ WARPLANES
THE C-130 HERCULES

JAN GOLDBERG

the rosen publishing group's
rosen
central

Published in 2003 by The Rosen Publishing Group, Inc.
29 East 21st Street, New York, NY 10010

Copyright © 2003 by The Rosen Publishing Group, Inc.

First Edition

Library of Congress Cataloging-in-Publication Data

Goldberg, Jan.
The C-130 Hercules / Jan Goldberg. — 1st ed.
    p. cm. — (U.S. warplanes)
Summary: Discusses the history of the C-130 Hercules transport plane and its use in military campaigns as well as civilian missions, such as studying weather, controlling fires, and supporting researchers in Antarctica.
Includes bibliographical references and index.
ISBN 0-8239-3873-5 (library binding)
1. Hercules (Turboprop transports)—Juvenile literature.
[1. Hercules (Turboprop transport) 2. Transport planes.]
I. Title. II. Series.
UG1242.T7G65 2003
623.7'465—dc21

2002010601

Manufactured in the United States of America

CONTENTS

During a time of peace, military supplies do not always need to be delivered immediately. Traveling to destinations by truck, ship, or train might work just fine. When battles are raging, however, these supplies must be delivered right away. Active armed forces must have enough food, supplies, medicine, and weapons to fulfill their mission's goals.

This is where transport planes like the C-130 are essential. Transport planes, also called cargo planes, are flown mostly by the United States Air Force, though the U.S. Navy and U.S. Marines also operate C-130s. They can deliver soldiers and supplies to the front lines as soon as they are needed.

Transport planes may not be the nicest looking planes in the air force. They are not sleek and modern looking, like fighter planes. Transport planes are big and bulky and often thought of as ugly. Their missions are rarely as dramatic as those of bombers. But if these planes were no longer able to fly their specialized missions, the rest of the military could not perform their important jobs. Transports help set the stage for all American military action by getting the troops and equipment into place quickly. The service these planes perform is one that cannot be minimized because it is crucial to military success and the security of the United States.

After nearly fifty years in production and numerous design changes and updated models, the C-130 Hercules has served in support of military operations and civilian emergency services. The C-130 shown above has been converted into a powerful fire-fighting weapon that can drop 3,000 gallons (11,356 liters) of special fire-retardant chemicals in only five seconds.

THE BIRTH OF THE HERCULES

The birth of the C-130 Hercules stemmed from an extremely important event that took place in 1950. War broke out between North Korea and South Korea. North Korea was supported by Communist China, while South Korea was backed by the United Nations (UN), an organization of nations from around the world that seeks to find peaceful solutions to armed conflicts and defends nations and ethnic or racial groups from hostile neighbors.

The United States is a member of the UN, so U.S. Army troops were sent to South Korea to help defend it against North Korean invasion. The U.S. military had two main transport planes in use at that time, the C-54 Skymaster and the C-124 Globemaster. While the Globemaster was capable of carrying 80,000 pounds (36,287 kg) of cargo or about 200 passengers, it was very slow. It could travel only 230 miles (370.15 kilometers) per hour.

It took the American military six long weeks to transport all their soldiers and equipment over to South Korea. This made the air force realize that it needed a better transport plane for the future—a new sort of plane that could bring large numbers of American troops and heavy loads of military equipment to trouble spots around the world quickly and efficiently.

Out of this need for speed and strength, the Hercules was born.

The Contest

In February 1951, the air force contacted four different airplane manufacturers—Boeing, McDonnell Douglas (today part of Boeing), Fairchild, and Lockheed (today called Lockheed Martin Aeronautics Company). It asked these companies to design a new transport

A C-124 Globemaster discharges its cargo—the fuselage of another plane. The C-124 first flew on November 24, 1949. Nicknamed "Old Shakey," it could carry 200 fully equipped troops or 123 wounded patients and their attendants. Although it was very reliable, it was also very slow. For instance, the C-124 took ninety-seven hours to get from Travis Air Force Base in California to South Vietnam and back. That's over four days!

plane that would satisfy a list of requirements. The air force wanted the new plane to have an interior similar to that of a railroad boxcar. The cargo floor had to be at the same level as the bed of the army's standard two-and-a-half-ton truck. This would make loading and unloading easier when the plane was on the ground and the truck backed up to its cargo bay. The plane had to have a ramp and rear door, and both needed to be functioning while the plane was in the air to allow parachute drops of soldiers and equipment. There had to be enough room inside the plane to carry ninety troops or sixty-four paratroopers (soldiers who parachute from the plane) for more than 2,500 miles (4,023 km) without refueling. The plane also had to be able to land on very short landing strips and on nearly any type of surface, including ice, snow, and sand.

The C-130 Hercules takes its first full flight on February 11, 1955. It was named after Hercules, who, in Greek mythology, is supposed to have been the strongest man on earth. The plane's engineers thought it would be impossible for anyone to design an aircraft that would fly higher, farther, and faster than any other transport plane. Today, over forty years later, the Lockheed C-130 Hercules is still rolling off the assembly line.

Experts in the military, and even in the aircraft industry, thought that there were too many requirements. They believed that such a plane would be nearly impossible to create, much less fly.

Lockheed's Winning Design

The four airplane manufacturers submitted their designs to the air force. On July 2, 1951, the air force announced the winner—Lockheed's L-206. The air force asked Lockheed to build two prototypes of the new plane. The Pentagon then changed the plane's name to C-130, as all air force cargo planes are given a *C* prefix. Lockheed referred to the C-130 as Hercules, in keeping with the company tradition of naming their planes after stars and constellations. Hercules is a northern constellation named after the mythical Greek hero famous for his great strength.

HERCS AROUND THE WORLD

In 1957, Australia became the first country aside from the United States to order the new plane from Lockheed. It ordered twelve C-130As for its Royal Australian Air Force. Other countries soon followed suit. Indonesia ordered ten, and Canada ordered four. Canada was so impressed with its new planes that it quickly ordered twenty-four more. In 1965, Britain's Royal Air Force ordered sixty-six Hercules planes. Nearly fifty years after its introduction, more than sixty-five countries around the world were flying the Herc.

Filling the First Order

Lockheed soon started working on the two prototypes at their California plant. They also built a full-scale wooden model of the plane. On August 23, 1954, the first test flight of a C-130 prototype was successfully completed. During this time, Lockheed executives decided that future C-130s would be built by Lockheed-Georgia, in Marietta, Georgia.

As a result, the engineers from California were all moved to Marietta. They started working on the air force's first order of seven airplanes. The first C-130 airplane was built and unveiled in Georgia on March 10, 1955. A month later, it completed its first flight. A total of 219 planes were ordered and Lockheed began to deliver them to the air force in late 1956.

The Formidable Herc

The Hercules is as tough as its name implies. This is only one of the reasons, however, that Lockheed's best-selling airplane has been so popular ever since its first appearance.

The Lockheed Company was known for building very modern, sleek airplanes. The C-130 Hercules, however, was very different from the other planes that it had designed. Everyone was surprised that the new plane was so big and bulky looking. Compared to the

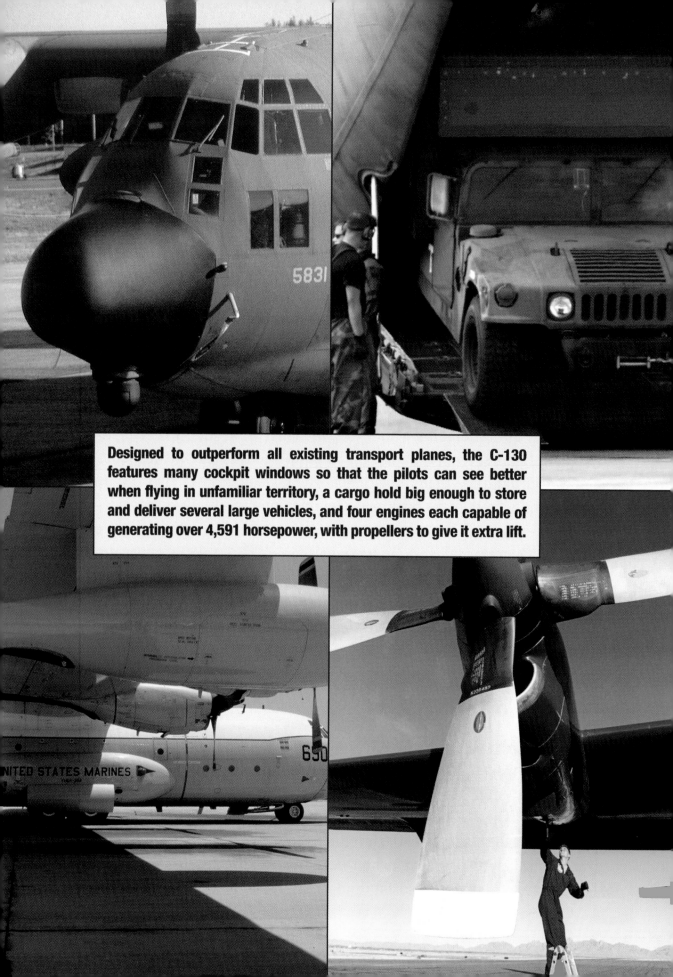

Designed to outperform all existing transport planes, the C-130 features many cockpit windows so that the pilots can see better when flying in unfamiliar territory, a cargo hold big enough to store and deliver several large vehicles, and four engines each capable of generating over 4,591 horsepower, with propellers to give it extra lift.

streamlined jets typical of Lockheed, the Hercules was considered very unattractive.

The C-130 was not designed with appearance in mind, however. It was designed to meet the air force's particular needs. The fuselage, or body, of the plane sat only 45 inches (1.1 meters) above the ground. When the rear cargo ramp was lowered, it was the same height as a truck bed, just as the air force requested.

The wing was set high atop the fuselage to insure that the propeller blades would clear the ground. This was especially important if the plane had to make a landing on rocky or bumpy ground. Low-slung propellers might strike the ground surface, damaging the blades or causing rocks and other debris to ricochet against the plane's body and wings.

The nose of the plane was rounded, not pointed like the more modern-looking planes. This gave it a snub-nosed appearance that, coupled with its size and closeness to the ground, made the plane look even more plodding. The cockpit had twenty-three separate window panels, giving the pilots excellent visibility when trying to land in an unfamiliar place. At an airport, pilots can rely on the ground crew to guide them and give them directions. A C-130 pilot often has no such luxury. When landing in a remote area, as C-130s often must, pilots need to be able to see all around the plane in order to maneuver safely and determine the best location for touching down.

The big and chunky shape of the fuselage was also necessary to make sure that the inside cargo bay could hold very large and heavy loads. The Hercules cargo bay is 40 feet (12.31 m) long, 10 feet (3.12 m) wide, and 9 feet (2.74 m) high. If you are five feet tall, for example, this means that eight people your height could lie head to toe inside the huge cargo bay.

Once the Hercules took to the skies and began performing its job, its critics quickly forgot about how unusual the plane looked.

Lockheed's incredible C-130 Hercules, also called the Herc, turned out to be everything the air force asked for and more. More than 2,200 Hercs have been built over the years, in more than seventy variations. Together, the 2,200 Hercs have recorded over two million hours of flight time. Most C-130s can stay in service for twenty-five years or longer, and over 1,600 are still in service today. It is easily Lockheed's most popular plane and its biggest success.

The View from the Outside

One C-130 Hercules consists of about 75,000 parts. As airplanes go, that is a fairly small number of parts. It is the plane's size and strength rather than its intricate features that make the Hercules so impressive.

The Hercules is 97 feet 9 inches (29.3 m) long, or about one-third the length of a football field! The Herc's wingspan, the length from one tip of the wing to the other, is even longer—132 feet 7 inches (39.7 m). The C-130 is 38 feet 3 inches (11.4 m) tall. That is about as high as a four-story building!

Amazingly, Lockheed did not just meet the air force's requirements for a new transport plane, it exceeded them. With a full load of cargo, the first C-130s could travel over 350 miles (560 kilometers) per hour. That was 20 percent faster than air force requirements. It also made the Hercules faster than the fastest passenger plane in service at the time. Over the years, the Herc's speed has only increased. The latest C-130 model, the C-130J, was introduced in 1999. It is able to travel more than 415 mph (664 km/hr).

The original Herc's rate of climb, or how fast it can gain elevation, was 55 percent faster than required by the air force. Its takeoff distance, the amount of runway it needs for acceleration before leaving the ground, was 25 percent less than required. These things have improved over time as well. The rate of climb for the C-130J is 50 percent faster than the first C-130s.

The Hercules was the first military transport plane to use turboprop engines instead of piston engines. A turboprop engine uses propellers. The propellers turn and produce thrust, or forward movement. Four T-56 turboprop engines, made by the Allison Engine Company of Indianapolis, Indiana, were chosen for the Hercules.

The propellers that were installed on the first Hercules airplanes had three blades. The pitch, or angle, of the blades was adjustable. Reversing the pitch would help the plane stop quickly or back up on short landing strips. Test pilots reported problems with these propellers, however. The pitch would sometimes change without warning, and that could be very dangerous. Lockheed searched for different propellers. Beginning with the C-130B models in 1958, the Hercules featured four-blade propellers made by a company named Hamilton-Standard. These propellers were used on all C-130 models until the introduction of the C-130J. In 1995, the Allison Engine Company became part of Rolls-Royce. The C-130J now uses Rolls-Royce AE2100D3 turboprop engines. The plane's propellers now have six blades each instead of four, helping to increase the plane's thrust and speed. They also weigh less and have fewer moving parts.

The Herc's large wing holds four internal fuel tanks. Together, these tanks hold nearly 6,000 gallons (22,712.5 liters) of gas. In addition, there are two external tanks mounted under the wings, each containing almost 1,300 gallons (4,921 liters). The Herc can carry enough fuel to travel more than 2,500 miles (4,000 km) without having to land. If the plane is empty of cargo, it can travel more than 5,000 miles (8,000 km) before running out of fuel.

This C-130, known as the MC-130 Combat Talon, has a high-speed aerial delivery system, in-flight refueling equipment, and a global positioning satellite navigation system, which allows it to fly through hostile airspace even in poor weather conditions. It can deliver supplies to precise drop zones as well as pick up troops and other military personnel. The Combat Talon was used in Operation Desert Storm and more recently in Operation Enduring Freedom.

The cockpit of a warplane, such as this KC-130 system, is more complicated than in average passenger jets. In addition to the many buttons and switches that are required to fly the aircraft, recent model KC-130s include many other dials to monitor the plane's defensive electronic and infrared countermeasures systems, a global positioning system, and night-vision lighting.

The View from the Inside

Starting at the front of the plane, we come first to the cockpit. As mentioned earlier, the large number of windows give the pilots good visibility and a panoramic view when trying to land in unfamiliar places. The cockpit is very roomy, so everyone has enough space to do their jobs. The navigation station and engineer's seat are right behind the pilots. In newer C-130 models, the cockpit has an upper and lower bunk, where crew members can rest between shifts. There is also a small galley, or kitchen. The rest room is at the rear of the plane.

The standard crew size of the C-130 is five: two pilots; a navigator, who sets and monitors the plane's course; a flight engineer, who is responsible for the plane's mechanical operation; and a loadmaster, who is in charge of the cargo. For more difficult missions, there might also be a second loadmaster. On especially long flights, longer than eighteen hours, there might be as many as nine or ten crew members. A large crew like this might include three or more pilots, two flight engineers, two navigators, and two loadmasters. This way, the crew can work in shifts and replace each other when they get tired. The minimum crew for the C-130 is four people. The latest model Herc, the C-130J, requires only a three-person crew.

Behind the cockpit is the large cargo bay. It is pressurized like the cockpit so that troops, hospital patients, and other passengers can breathe normally even at high altitudes. For passenger comfort, it has air conditioning and heating. The air conditioning also protects perishable supplies, like food and medicine.

Different models of the Hercules can carry different amounts of cargo and troops. Most C-130s have a cargo bay the size of a railroad boxcar: 40 feet (12.31 m) long, 10 feet (3.12 m) wide, and 9 feet (2.74 m) tall. That is enough room to carry ninety-two troops, sixty-four paratroopers, or seventy-four patients on stretchers and two medical attendants. Troops sit on seats made of webbing that line the two long sides of the cargo bay. On some Hercules models, including the new C-130J-30, the cargo compartment was expanded. On these planes, the cargo bay is 55 feet (16.9 m) long instead of 40 feet (12.31 m) long.

When carrying cargo, the C-130 can hold as much as four jeeps, four trailers, and five cargo pallets. Cargo pallets are platforms that hold boxed materials. Depending on the model, the Herc's entire load of cargo and passengers can weigh anywhere from 30,000 pounds (13,608 kg) to more than 45,000 pounds (20,412 kg). The total operating weight of the Herc, including the plane, fuel, crew, and cargo, ranges from 155,000 pounds (70,307 kg) to 175,000 pounds (79,379 kg).

On each side of the airplane fuselage there are two doors. This is where the paratroopers can parachute out of the plane. At the rear of the plane is the loading ramp. When the plane is on the ground, the ramp is lowered all the way down for loading and unloading. Rollers can be installed on the cargo bay's floor to allow for quick and easy sliding on

STANDARD VERSIONS OF THE HERC

★ **C-130A:** The original production model that was initiated in 1951 and joined the air force in 1956. It featured four Allison T56-A-11 turbo-prop engines. The initial order was for 219 planes, which were used as freighters, assault transports, and ambulances.

★ **C-130B:** Entered the air force in 1959 and featured upgraded Allison T56-A-7 turboprop engines. The C-130B carried additional fuel in its wings and had strengthened landing gear. Today they are used primarily in aerial fire-fighting missions.

★ **C-130D:** These are C-130As modified to feature wheel-ski landing gear for use in the Arctic and the Antarctic. The D model also has greater fuel capacity.

★ **C-130E:** First delivered to the air force in 1962. C-130Es are a modification of the C-130B with two underwing fuel tanks and an increased range (the distance it can fly before refueling). They now feature the self-contained navigation system (SCNS), which allows for easier navigation, especially in low-altitude situations. They also include an improved autopilot that helps reduce the chance of collisions.

★ **C-130H:** First delivered to the air force in 1974. C-130Hs feature updated T-56-A-T5 turboprop engines and increased fuel capacity. In 1993, the night vision instrumentation system was introduced. In addition to military applications, the C-130Hs are also used to fight fires, suppress insect-borne epidemics by aerial spraying of insecticide, and support Arctic and Antarctic operations.

★ **C-130J:** First delivered to Britain's Royal Air Force in 1999. Because of the improved Allison AE2100D3 engines and Dowty R391 propellers, the C-130J climbs faster, higher, and farther than older Hercs. It can also take off and land in a shorter distance.

and off of the cargo pallets. If tanks and other vehicles are being transported, the cargo bay must have a flat surface. In this case, the rollers can be removed. Sometimes, supplies must be unloaded while the plane is in the air. The rear door can be partially lowered and the supplies air-dropped. Parachutes attached to the cargo help it fall slowly and land safely with a minimum of impact.

One of the C-130's best assets is its versatility. It has been used successfully for nearly every kind of military operation possible, including dropping troops and equipment into hostile areas, aerial refueling of planes and helicopters, reconnaissance (aerial exploration of territory), and dropping of food and other basic supplies to refugees fleeing war zones.

Tactical Airlift and Emergency Evacuation

Tactical airlift means transporting troops, supplies, weapons, and other equipment to wherever they are needed, often at the front lines of a conflict. This is the type of mission for which the Hercules was specifically designed. The plane might need to carry soldiers and their gear right into the middle of a war. Sometimes there is no safe place to land. Other times, it is too dangerous to land because it might alert the enemy to the troop's presence. In this case, the soldiers and equipment have to be parachuted out of the plane down to the ground.

In addition to dropping soldiers into war zones, the plane might also need to pick up soldiers who have completed a mission and bring them safely home. Or injured soldiers or civilians might need to be airlifted out of a war zone during a mission. They are loaded onto the Hercules, given in-flight emergency care (if a medical staff is on board), and transported to a safe place where they can receive medical attention.

When equipment is being transported, there are three main methods of aerial delivery. In the first method, parachutes pull the load—which can weigh up to 42,000 pounds (19,051 kg)—from the back of the airplane. When the load is safely away from the plane, cargo parachutes inflate. Slowly and gently, the cargo is lowered to the ground.

The C-130 Hercules can make precision drops thanks to its low altitude parachute extraction system (LAPES). The air force uses the C-130 to make drops of tools, equipment, and medical supplies in dangerous situations. The parachutes ensure that the supplies being delivered are dropped relatively gently and come to a stop within a short distance.

The second method is called the container delivery system (CDS). With this system, the bundles of supplies are pulled by the force of their weight and gravity. Each bundle may weigh up to 2,200 pounds (998 kg). Once they are clear of the aircraft, parachutes inflate and take them to the ground.

The third method is called the low altitude parachute extraction system (LAPES). This method was designed for the heaviest loads—up to 38,000 pounds (17,237 kg)—which would either be too heavy for the parachutes or would hit the ground too hard, possibly resulting in damage to the cargo. When the plane is flying only five or ten feet above the ground, large inflated cargo parachutes pull the load out. With the help of these parachutes, the load slides to a stop within a very short distance.

OPERATIONS DESERT SHIELD AND DESERT STORM

Operations Desert Shield and Desert Storm were part of a multinational effort led by the United States to drive Iraqi invaders out of the tiny Persian Gulf nation of Kuwait. More than 145 Hercs were used in this effort. Their main responsibility was to bring troops to bases near the front lines. Yet their mission also included providing supplies to bases and evacuating wounded soldiers. The Hercs flew more than 46,500 sorties, or individual flights—as many as 500 a day—and moved more than 209,000 people and 300,000 tons of supplies.

Flying Gas Station

The Hercules is often used to refuel other planes while both are in flight. This "flying gas station" attaches itself to the other plane with a long hose. Once the two planes are linked together, the Herc pumps fuel to the other plane through the hose.

C-130s that are used for refueling are given the prefix *K* (which stands for kerosene, an aviation fuel). The fuel comes from the two exterior tanks under the wings. An extra fuel tank can also be carried in the cargo compartment. It holds an additional 3,600 gallons (13,627.5 l) of fuel. With its four internal fuel tanks, two external fuel tanks, and the extra tank in the cargo hold, the KC-130 can hold about 13,800 gallons (52,239 l) of fuel.

KC-130s are used primarily by the marines. These planes can transfer gas to other planes and helicopters at a rate of 300 gallons (1,135.6 l) per minute. They can even fill two different airplanes at once. The KC-130 is also used by the marines to perform many other common C-130 missions, such as troop and equipment transport.

Gunships

C-130 planes with the prefix *A* (standing for attack) are used as gunships. These Hercules aircraft are heavily armed with weapons, such as cannons and mounted guns, that fire from the port, or left, side of the plane at targets on the ground or in the air. Special sensors and radar equipment allow the plane to quickly locate targets and tell the difference between friendly and enemy forces. This minimizes the chance of friendly fire, which is an accidental attack on one's own troops. These planes require a large crew, including four gunners. A gunner is a soldier who is trained in firing the weapons.

The Hercules serves as a flying gas station, refueling helicopters and other planes in midair.

Electronic Warfare

Hercules airplanes equipped for electronic warfare are called Commando Solo and given the prefix *EC* for electronic combat. These planes operate like flying radio and television stations. They have cassette recorders, video recorders, TV monitors, transmitters, and a live microphone. With all this equipment, crews can interrupt a country's normal TV or radio broadcasts and transmit their own messages to viewers and listeners.

The EC-130 played an important role in Operation Enduring Freedom, the multinational offensive against terrorist fighters and their camps in Afghanistan following the September 11 attacks against the United States. The Al Qaeda terrorist group, led by Osama bin Laden and backed by the Taliban, an Islamic fundamentalist government, were thought to be responsible for the attacks on the World Trade Center in New York City and the Pentagon in Arlington, Virginia, (just outside Washington, D.C.), which killed thousands of civilians.

Al Qaeda members and Taliban officials were the targets of the operation, but they represented only a small percentage of the Afghan people. Allied forces wanted to protect innocent Afghans from harm and possibly enlist their help. According to Harold Kennedy of *National Defense* magazine, EC-130s broadcast this message to Afghan civilians during Operation Enduring Freedom in late 2001, warning them to avoid areas that would soon be under attack: "We have no wish to hurt you, the innocent people of Afghanistan. Stay away from military installations, government buildings, terrorist camps, roads, factories, or bridges." The EC-130 also dropped millions of

This 105 mm Howitzer is able to fire multiple rounds from a special "feed." It is only one of several weapons (including a 40 mm cannon) used by the AC-130 Spectre (or Spooky).

leaflets in Afghanistan in 2001 and 2002. Some offered a $25 million reward for Osama bin Laden. Others urged the Afghans to "stop fighting for the Taliban and live." Millions of packets of food were dropped to the Afghans as well, along with cooking and preparing instructions. Another type of Herc devoted to electronic warfare is the EC-130H Compass Call, used for battlefield communications and other top-secret military tasks.

Special Operations

C-130 airplanes with the prefix *M* are used by the special operations forces of all branches of the U.S. armed forces and given the nickname Combat Talon. Combat Talon planes have a global positioning system,

OPERATION ENDURING FREEDOM

As in every other conflict in its fifty-year history, the Hercules played a star role in Afghanistan while also keeping a low profile. Its missions in support of Operation Enduring Freedom included:

★ Dropping Army Ranger paratroopers in advance of a raid on a Taliban airfield in southern Afghanistan

★ Dropping millions of leaflets offering rewards for terrorist leaders (including $25 million for Osama bin Laden) and warning of the dangers of unexploded bombs

★ Pounding enemy targets with cannons and mounted guns.

★ Broadcasting radio programs, music, and announcements urging Afghans to withdraw their support of the Taliban and Al Qaeda forces

★ Refueling special operations helicopters that flew deep into Afghanistan

★ Delivering emergency supplies such as food, water, tents, and blankets to starving and freezing Afghan refugees stranded in the mountains as winter approached

which is a guidance system that receives precise information on a target's location from satellites. This technology helps the MC-130s land or airdrop troops and supplies within very small zones with great accuracy. Their special terrain-following radar allows them to fly very close to the ground without hitting any unexpected hills, buildings, or other obstructions. Many of their missions are covert, or highly secretive, and involve the delivery of troops behind enemy lines.

Search and Rescue

C-130s used in search and rescue missions over land or water are given the prefix *H*. These missions are usually designed to find lost, stranded, wounded, or captured soldiers and bring them back to safety. HC-130s can help directly with the mission, or they can provide in-flight refueling for search and rescue helicopters.

HC-130s often fly their missions at night. They are able to operate without using their external lights. They can also fly without communications of any kind. This helps them to avoid radar detection in hostile areas. The crew uses special night-vision goggles (NVGs) so they can see in the dark.

The standard HC-130 crew size is usually ten. There are two pilots, a navigator, a flight engineer, a communications specialist, two loadmasters, and three paratroopers. The paratroopers, who may parachute into hostile territory to find and save injured or captured American soldiers, are specially trained in emergency medical treatment and survival techniques.

A C-130 Hercules from the Wyoming National Guard drops 3,000 gallons of water on a forest fire burning on Mount Arjuna near Surabaya, Indonesia, in October 1997.

Not only is the C-130 the most successful, versatile, and popular military transport plane in history, it has also proven its usefulness in many civilian missions. The Herc has boldly flown into the eyes of hurricanes to gather forecast information. It has raced to fight fires around the world, helping to contain blazes that threatened precious forests and parkland. It has even helped sustain small communities of research scientists in what may be the most remote corner of the world—Antarctica.

Weather Reconnaissance

Though the term "reconnaissance" often refers to the secret investigation of enemy territory, it can also mean any sort of survey or investigation that seeks to gather facts. Beginning in 1959, special equipment for investigating weather conditions was added to the C-130. This plane is called the WC-130. It was given the W prefix to stand for "weather" and nicknamed the Hurricane Hunter.

Scientists at the National Hurricane Center in Miami, Florida, decide when to send the Hurricane Hunters out to investigate weather conditions that indicate the possible development of dangerous and destructive hurricanes. A tropical storm is a weather system that may become a hurricane if it gains enough strength. When a tropical storm forms over the ocean, scientists need to find out exactly how powerful the storm is and how likely it is to develop into a dangerous hurricane. They also try to determine if the storm is headed toward the shore, threatening people and property. The information they receive from the WC-130s will generate weather forecasts and determine if severe-weather warnings or even evacuations are necessary.

Because the WC-130 Hercules operates well in difficult weather conditions, it is used for tracking weather for both military and civilian purposes. For this reason, it is also known as the Hurricane Hunter.

The crew on board a WC-130 is a little different from the standard C-130 crew. Like a standard crew, there are two pilots, a navigator, and a flight engineer. There is also a meteorologist, a scientist who studies weather, and a systems operator who monitors the weather equipment.

Weather reconnaissance missions can cover almost 3,500 miles (5,633 km) and can take from ten to fifteen hours to complete. During this time, the plane flies right into the eye, or center, of a hurricane several times to gather data such as wind speed and direction, humidity, air pressure, and temperature. To accomplish this, the WC-130 uses sensors installed on the outside of the plane and a data-gathering cylinder that is attached to a parachute and dropped straight into the hurricane. The information that is collected is sent immediately to the National Hurricane Center via satellite.

Use of the WC-130 planes has improved hurricane forecasting by 30 percent or more. This is important because evacuating people along the coastline can be very expensive. Evacuation can cost as much as a million dollars per mile of evacuated land. Therefore, accurate information about the severity and path of a hurricane is necessary before evacuation can begin. Early warnings of the type a WC-130 provides can also serve an even more valuable function—the saving of hundreds of lives.

Fighting Fires Around the World

When a forest fire is raging out of control, it can be very difficult for firefighters on the ground to put it out. It is especially difficult if the fire is very large or if it is in a remote, hard-to-reach location, such as on top of a mountain. In circumstances like this, C-130 Hercules planes modified with special fire-fighting equipment can quickly come to the rescue.

The Modular Airborne Fire Fighting System (MAFFS)—a machine that stores and releases fire retardant—was made especially for the Hercules. MAFFS was designed by the U.S. Forest Service. With MAFFS, an Air National Guard Hercules can be temporarily converted into an air tanker. The MAFFS unit slides up the ramp and into the rear door of the cargo bay. Two large pipes hang out the open cargo door. Pressurized air forces fire-retardant slurry out of the pipes and onto the fire. Slurry is a mixture of water, clay, and fertilizer. It is about the same color and thickness as tomato sauce.

Once dropped into the path of the fire, the slurry sticks to the trees, leaves, and dead wood in the fire's path and helps to make them resistant to the flames. One MAFFS tank holds 3,000 gallons (11,356 l) of slurry. At the fastest flow rate, the entire 3,000 gallons can be dropped onto the fire in just five seconds.

Fighting fires has always been a dangerous job and is no less so when done from high above the flames. On June 17, 2002, a C-130A operated by the National Interagency Fire Center crashed while battling a wildfire in northern California. Just after making a pass over the fire,

HERCS TO THE RESCUE!

In 1997, ninety-six members of the Wyoming Air National Guard flew their Hercules planes to Indonesia. They helped fight a large jungle fire burning on the island of Sumatra. This guard unit is one of only four in the United States qualified to fly these fire-fighting missions. The U.S. Forest Service also has several C-130 planes of its own. These planes are equipped with a fire-fighting system, too, but it is not as advanced as MAFFS.

the plane's wings snapped off and flames erupted as the fuselage spiraled to the ground. All three people on board were killed.

Support in Antarctica

The continent of Antarctica is home to the South Pole and more than 90 percent of the ice in the world. It is also the temporary home of the scientists who travel there each year to do research. They study the sea life, such as whales and penguins, and natural features, such as Mount Erebus, an active volcano. They also study the weather and the ice that covers the continent, which can be as much as two miles thick. Many researchers get to Antarctica with the help of a special plane on skis—a C-130 Hercules with the prefix *L*. Once there, most of the scientists' supplies and provisions are supplied by LC-130s, which fly to various research stations around the frozen continent.

The LC-130 is the largest aircraft ever to be fitted with ski-wheels. The skis are retractable, which means they can be pulled up and out of the way when they are not needed. The main skis are twenty feet (six m) long and five feet five inches (1.67 m) wide. They weigh about 2,000 pounds (907 kg) each. The ski under the plane's nose is the same width, but it is only ten feet (3 m) long. The ski-wheels allow the Hercules to land on snow and ice.

An LC-130 sits on snowy McMurdo military base in the Antarctic. It is equipped with retractable ski-wheels that allow it to land on the frozen ground. The LC-130 is able to drop off or pick up scientists and their equipment in remote regions of the Arctic and the Antarctic, and perform evacuations.

CONCLUSION

The C-130 Hercules has been in production longer than any other airplane. For more than fifty years, it has flown almost every possible military mission. It is a very important part of aviation history and military history, but what is its likely future? Will the Herc still play such a major role in military and civilian missions around the world in the twenty-first century?

Lockheed Martin, the plane's manufacturer, certainly hopes so. In order to insure its future role in the U.S. armed forces, it has worked hard to improve the Hercules still further. The result is a new model, the C-130J. The C-130J looks just like the trusty old Herc on the outside, but it is new and improved on the inside (though even louder than its noisy predecessors). Compared to earlier models, its maximum speed is 21 percent greater, thanks to new engines and six-blade propellers that provide 29 percent greater thrust and 15 percent greater fuel efficiency. Its climb time is down 50 percent, while its cruising altitude is 40 percent higher and its range 40 percent farther. The Herc can now reach 28,000 feet (8,534.4 m) in fourteen minutes and can take off and land in a shorter distance. It also features special radar and imaging equipment that make it easier and safer to operate at very low altitudes.

Particularly attractive to the air force is the fact that maintenance and operating costs of the new Hercs are expected to decrease by as much as 45 percent. Earlier C-130 models required more than twenty maintenance hours per flight hour. The C-130Js are expected to require only ten hours or less of maintenance per flight hour.

Most important, the newest generation of C-130s is still able to perform the wide variety of missions that has made the Hercules so popular. In fact, the C-130Js will be available as weather (WC), electronic combat (EC), and fuel tanker (KC) configured aircraft. The KC-130J in

particular has greatly benefited from the upgrades. It will now be able to refuel planes and helicopters midair while traveling faster than earlier Hercules models. Older Hercs could deliver fuel while flying at 115 mph (185 km/h); the KC-130J will be able to perform the same operation at 310.5 mph (499.7 km/h). It will also be able to offload, or pump fuel into planes and helicopters far more quickly than older Hercs could.

An additional stretched version of the C-130J is also available. The C-130J-30 is 15 feet (4.6 m) longer than the C-130J, increasing the storage space of the cargo hold. When loaded with 35,000 pounds (15,876 kg) of cargo, it has a 3,269 mile (5,261 km) range. In comparison, the C-130J has a 3,062 mile (4,928 km) range and older Hercs only about 2,000 miles (3,218.7 km). Despite its size, the stretched Herc is roughly as fast as the C-130J, flying over 400 mph (643.7 km/hr). Older Hercs flew at roughly 350 mph (563.3 km/hr).

C-130 pilots train in simulators, such as the one shown here, to avoid both injury to the trainee and damage to the expensive aircraft. The cockpit of this C-130J Hercules simulator mirrors that of the actual plane. A series of hydraulic systems upon which the equipment is mounted simulate the plane's motion.

Currently, the air force has acquired twelve C-130Js as replacements for the older EC-130s and HC-130s. The C-130J program may be expanded to allow for the acquisition of twelve Hercs a year.

Fifty years after the air force requested designs for a new transport plane, the Hercules still seems to have a lot of life left in it. C-130s have put in a combined total of twenty million flight hours. Over the last

THE C-130J AT A GLANCE

Primary Function: Tactical airlift.

Contractor: Lockheed Martin Aeronautics Company.

Engines: Four Rolls-Royce AE 2100D3 turboprops.

Length: 97 feet 9 inches (29.3 m).

Height: 38 feet 3 inches (11.4 m).

Wingspan: 132 feet 7 inches (39.7 m).

Standard Cargo Compartment: Length: 40 feet (12.31 m); Width: 119 inches (3.12 m); Height: 9 feet (2.74 m).

Rear Ramp: Length: 123 inches (3.12 m); Width: 119 inches (3.02 m).

Speed: 417 mph (667 km/hr) at 22,000 feet (6,706 m) of altitude.

Ceiling (maximum altitude): 33,000 feet (10,000 m) with 45,000 pounds (17,716 kg) of cargo.

Maximum Allowable Payload (including cargo, passengers, and weapons): 46,631 pounds (21,151 kg).

Range with 35,000 pounds (15,876 km) of Payload: 3,062 miles (4,928 km).

Maximum Load: 6 cargo pallets, 16 CDS bundles, 74 wounded soldiers on stretchers, 92 combat troops, or 64 paratroopers.

Minimum Crew: Two pilots and a loadmaster. Aeromedical evacuation missions require an additional medical crew of one flight nurse and two medical technicians.

Cost Per Plane: $48.5 million.

Date Deployed: February 1999.

thirty years, 900 Hercs have been delivered to the air force, and C-130s also serve in the armed services of over sixty foreign countries. The mighty Herc is expected to remain in production well into the twenty-first century.

A C-130J airplane being assembled at a Lockheed Martin factory in Marietta, Georgia. Each C-130J costs about $48.5 million and takes about fourteen months to assemble. The "J" model features improved engines, propellers, armor, and avionics.

The Next Big Thing?

Will any other military transport plane ever be able to compete with the success of the C-130? The Boeing Company would answer yes. Boeing's research and development unit is called Phantom Works. Engineers at Phantom Works are currently designing a new transport plane. They call it the Advanced Theater Transport (ATT).

The ATT looks very modern. It does not have a tail. Its propellers have eight blades instead of six. The wingspan and length of the plane are less than those of a C-130, but the fuselage is almost twice as wide. Boeing wanted to design a plane that will be able to take off and land on airstrips much shorter than the Herc needs. Boeing believes that the new plane will be able to carry 80,000 to 100,000 pounds

A C-130 Hercules in flight. The C-130 is perhaps the most versatile warplane in the United States's military arsenal. Its invaluable uses in airlift, weather reconnaissance, and refueling, its prowess as a gunship, and its adaptability to new tasks may ensure its survival in today's fast-paced era of technological development.

(36,287 to 45,359 kg) of cargo—roughly twice as much as the C-130 can haul over a distance of 3,450 miles (5,552 km).

In addition, the German company Airbus Industrie has begun development of its own military transporter, the Airbus A400M. It had been designed to meet the requirements of the air forces of Belgium, France, Germany, Italy, Spain, Turkey, and the United Kingdom. The A400M will be able to take off and land from unprepared landing strips without any ground support. It will have in-flight refueling capability and be able to be converted into an aerial tanker. It will feature excellent low-speed handling characteristics necessary for the air dropping of troops and cargo. The A400M's cargo hold will be 75 feet (22.9 m) long, 13 feet (4 m) wide, and 12 feet 7 inches (3.85 m) high. Its maximum speed will be 534 mph (859 km/hr), with a range of between 4,082 to 5,635 miles (6,569 to 9,068 km) and a maximum load of 81,571 pounds (37,000 kg) or 120 troops.

Boeing and Airbus hope that the ATT or A400M will eventually replace the C-130 Hercules. This might happen one day in the future, if these other planes are able to do everything the companies plan. After such a long and successful history, however, an airplane as popular and reliable as the C-130 will not just disappear from service overnight. The C-130J and future models will be carrying on the legendary Hercules name for many more years to come. According to Lockheed Martin, "The 20th century's greatest airlifter will also be the 21st century's greatest."

GLOSSARY

clearance   The distance by which one object clears another or the clear space between them.

contract   A written or spoken agreement to deliver products or services.

loadmaster   The person aboard a cargo aircraft who is responsible for the cargo, including the loading and unloading procedures. Loadmasters are also responsible for the safety of the cargo during transport.

pallet   A portable platform for storing and transporting loads of cargo.

paratroopers   Troops equipped with parachutes so they can be dropped from an aircraft.

perishable   Food or other goods that can spoil quickly, often because of extreme heat or cold.

piston engine   An engine that uses cylinders containing pistons. The piston is the disc (or smaller cylinder) that moves up and down inside the slightly larger cylinder, generating energy.

prefix   A letter, syllable, or word at the beginning of another word meant to change the meaning of the original word.

prototype   A trial model, pattern, or preliminary version.

refugee   A person seeking to escape from a war or natural disaster.

rugged   Strong and sturdy, especially in bodily structure or construction.

unveil   To make public for the first time.

FOR MORE INFORMATION

In the United States

Air Combat Command
Public Affairs Office
115 Thompson Street, Suite 211
Langley AFB, VA 23665-1987
(757) 764-5014
Web site: http://www2.acc.af.mil

Air Force Historical Research Agency
600 Chennault Circle
Building 1405
Maxwell AFB, AL 36112-6424
(334) 953-2395
Web site: http://www.au.af.mil/au/afhra

Air Force Research Laboratory
Public Affairs Office
1864 4th Street
Building 15, Room 225
Wright-Patterson AFB, OH 45433-7131
Web site: http://www.afrl.af.mil

Air Mobility Command
Public Affairs Office
503 Ward Drive, Suite 214
Scott AFB, IL 62225-5335

Naval Air Systems Command
Public Affairs Department
47123 Buse Road, Unit IPT
Building 2272, Suite 075
Patuxent River, MD 20670-5440
(301) 757-1487

Smithsonian National Air and Space Museum
7th and Independence Avenue SW
Washington, DC 20560
Web site: http://www.nasm.si.edu

United States Air Force (USAF)
Public Affairs Resource Library
1690 Air Force Pentagon
Washington, DC 20330-1690
Web site: http://www.af.mil

USAF Academy
Director of Cadet Admissions
2304 Cadet Drive, Suite 200
Colorado Springs, CO 80840-5025
Web site: http://www.usafa.af.mil

USAF Air Education and Training Command (AETC)
Public Affairs Office
Randolph AFB, TX 78150
(210) 652-4400
Web site: http://www.aetc.randolph.af.mil

USAF Museum
1100 Spaatz Street
Wright-Patterson AFB, OH 45433
(937) 255-3286
Web site: http://www.wpafb.af.mil/museum/index.htm

In Canada

Air Force Association of Canada
P.O. Box 2460, Station "D"
Ottawa, ON K1P 5W6
(613) 992-7482
Web site: http://www.airforce.ca

Department of National Defence
National Defence Headquarters
Major-General George R. Pearkes Building
101 Colonel By Drive
Ottawa, ON K1A 0K2
(613) 995-2534
Web site: http://www.forces.ca/eng/index.html

Royal Canadian Air Force (RCAF)
Director Air Force Public Affairs
NDHQ Major-General George R. Pearkes Building
12 NT, 101 Colonel By Drive
Ottawa, ON K1A 0K2
Web site: http://www.airforce.dnd.ca/index_e.htm

RCAF Memorial Museum
P.O. Box 1000, Station Forces
Astra, ON K0K 3W0
(613) 965-2140
Web site: http://www.rcafmuseum.on.ca

Royal Military College of Canada
P.O. Box 17000, Station Forces
Kingston, ON K7K 7B4
(613) 541-6000
Web site: http://www.rmc.ca

Web Sites

Due to the changing nature of Internet links, the Rosen Publishing Group, Inc., has developed an online list of Web sites related to the subject of this book. This site is updated regularly. Please use this link to access the list:

http://www.rosenlinks.com/usw/herc/

FOR FURTHER READING

Baysura, Kelly. *Cargo Planes*. Vero Beach, FL: Rourke Enterprises, Inc., 2001.

Bowman, Martin W. *Lockheed C-130 Hercules.* Wiltshire, England: Crowood Press, Ltd., 1999.

Dabney, Joseph Earl. *Herk: Hero of the Skies.* Marietta, GA: Larlin Corp., 1986.

Emert, Phyllis Rabin. *Transports and Bombers.* Englewood Cliffs, NJ: Julian Messner, 1990.

Gunston, Bill. *American Warplanes*. London: Salamander Books, Ltd., 1997.

Jarrett, Philip. *Ultimate Aircraft.* New York: Dorling Kindersley Publishing, Inc., 2000.

Johnstone, Michael. *Planes.* New York: Dorling Kindersley Publishing, Inc., 1994.

Smith, Peter Charles. *Lockheed C-130 Hercules: The World's Favourite Military Transport.* Salop, England: Airlife Publishing, Ltd., 2002.

Verlinden, Francois. *Lock on No. 3: Lockheed C-130 Hercules.* O'Fallon, MO: Verlinden Productions, Inc., 1986.

BIBLIOGRAPHY

Baker, David. *Airlift* (Military Aircraft Series). Vero Beach, FL: Rourke Enterprises, Inc., 1989.

Chant, Christopher. *An Illustrated Data Guide to Modern Reconnaissance Aircraft.* Twickenham, England: Tiger Books International, 1997.

Federation of American Scientists. "C-130 Hercules." February 2000. Retrieved April 2002 (http://www.fas.org/man/dod-101/sys/ac/c-130.htm).

Francillon, Rene J. *Lockheed Aircraft Since 1913.* London: Putnam & Company, Ltd., 1982.

Gaines, Mike. *Hercules.* New York: Jane's Publishing, Inc., 1984.

Jarrett, Philip. *Ultimate Aircraft.* New York: Dorling Kindersley Publishing, Inc., 2000.

Johnstone, Michael. *Planes.* New York: Dorling Kindersley Publishing, Inc., 1994.

Kennedy, Harold. "Why Special Ops Prefer C-130s for Many Missions." *National Defense*. April 2002. Retrieved May 2002 (http://www.nationaldefensemagazine.org/article.cfm?Id=723).

Kinzey, Bert, and Ray Leader. *Colors and Markings: Special Purpose C-130 Hercules.* New York: McGraw-Hill Professional Publishing, 1987.

McGowan, Sam. *C-130 Hercules: Tactical Airlift Missions, 1956–1975.* New York: McGraw-Hill Professional Publishing, 1988.

Morris, M. *C-130: The Hercules.* Novato, CA: Presidio Press, 1988.

Neely, Mike. "Lockheed C-130 Hercules." *The Aviation Zone*. 1997–2002. Retrieved May 2002 (http://www.theaviationzone.com/facts/c130.htm).

Reed, Chris. *Lockheed C-130 Hercules and Its Variants.* Atglen, PA: Schiffer Publishing, Ltd., 1999.

Rendall, David. *Jane's Aircraft Recognition Guide.* Glasgow: HarperCollins Publishers, 1996.

USAF Fact Sheet. "C-130 Hercules." July 2001. Retrieved April 2002 (http://www.af.mil/news/factsheets/C_130_Hercules.html).

INDEX

Operation Enduring Freedom,
    22–23, 24

P

paratroopers, 7, 17, 24, 25, 34
Pentagon, 8, 22
pilot, 11, 13, 16, 17, 25, 28, 34
propellers, 11, 13, 18, 32

R

refueling, 19, 21, 24, 25, 33
Rolls-Royce, 13, 34

S

search and rescue, 25
September 11, 2001, terrorist attacks, 22
special operations, 23–25

T

tactical airlift, 19, 34
Taliban, 22–23, 24
turboprop engines, 13, 18, 34

U

United States Air Force, 5, 6–11,
    12, 33
United States Army, 6, 7
United States Forest Service, 29, 31
United States Marines, 5, 21
United States Navy, 5

W

WC-130, 27–29
weather reconnaissance, 27–29, 32

CREDITS

About the Author

Jan Goldberg is an experienced educator and the author of thirty-five nonfiction books and hundreds of educational articles, textbooks, and other projects.

Photo Credits

Cover, pp. 4, 10 (top left), 16, 23, 36 © David Halford; p. 7 © Hulton/Archive/Getty Images, Inc.; pp. 8, 30 © Bettmann/Corbis; pp. 10 (top right and bottom right), 24, 26 © AP/Wide World Photos; pp. 10 (bottom left), 14–15, 22, 28 © George Hall/Corbis; p. 20 © U.S. Air Force; p. 33 © Senior Airman Jess Harvey/U.S. Air Force; p. 35 © Jim McDonald/Corbis.

Layout and Design

Tom Forget